Invitation

to

Life...

A PLEDGE TRAINING MANUAL
FOR
MEMBERS OF BETA SIGMA PHI

LARGE PRINT EDITION

Walter W. Ross & Co., Inc.
1800 West 91st Place, Kansas City, Missouri 64114
Printed in U.S.A.

816/444-6800 FAX: 816/333-6206
www.betasigmaphi.org

Dedicated...

To you, the friendliest, the loveliest-minded, and the most socially respected—the members of Beta Sigma Phi.

Walter W. Ross
Founder
Beta Sigma Phi

Foreword

Standing in the darkness as an initiate, you heard the ritual of Beta Sigma Phi. It was, and is, an invitation to life. This program, designed for the months of your pledge training program, is to assist you in accepting fully that invitation. Your sole contribution to the sum of things is yourself. The invitation we give you is to life as an art, to make of your own life a work of art, a masterpiece of Beauty, Love, and Truth.

The Picture of the beautiful is always complete and can be glimpsed in one moment of perfect vision. But the labor of applying the paint to the canvas, arranging the color and line, creating the design, and composing the details is a life-work for the devout craftsman

It is this high occupation with which you are to be concerned in your chapter life. Your ideas are your life portrait seen in advance. The only choice is in the kind of life one would care to spend one's effort on.

This outline, and the ones to follow, are planned to develop the membership into a widening consciousness of the life beautiful, and to freer usage of our creative energies.

The consistent and faithful use of these programs will distinguish you as a true Beta Sigma Phi.

SPECIAL MESSAGE
FOR VICE-PRESIDENTS

HOW TO USE THIS BOOK

Invitation to Life and the *Book of Beta Sigma Phi* are the basic references for pledge training. The success of pledge training will depend to some extent on how well the vice-president follows the intention of these books.

The books are designed to take advantage of "programmed instruction" techniques. Pledges should be assigned to read and study the subject of the next meeting.

The subject will be discussed at the appropriate meeting and questions will be answered at the end of the discussion.

This gives the vice-president the opportunity to correct any misinformation or misconception which is discovered in the answers given by the pledges.

The basic effort will be for each pledge to read the material assigned. It will be assigned in one meeting and discussed at the next meeting. The discussion will amplify and clarify what she has read. By using this system, each meeting will become a discussion meeting.

At the end of approximately six months, a new member will have completed her training and fulfilled the pledge training requirements for her next degree.

Some of the rituals for Beta Sigma Phi are contained in this book. It should be assigned for the pledges to read as soon as they have received their copies of Invitation to Life and before the first pledge training meeting.

SUGGESTIONS FOR
PLEDGE TRAINING MEETINGS

As vice-president, you (or a pledge trainer if appointed) are in charge of pledge trainer meetings which should be held as follows.

In a newly organized chapter pledge training should be held as part of each regular meeting.

In an established chapter, pledge training may be held at a time other than the regular meeting hours (but it may be on the same night, during or after the meeting). Training should take place at least once a month and, if practical, twice a month.

Like any Beta Sigma Phi meeting, pledge training should be enjoyable as well as productive. Make every effort to get a good discussion going and to carefully answer all questions pledges ask. DO NOT RELY ON YOUR MEMORY TO ANSWER THIR QUESTIONS. REFER TO THE BOOK OF BETA SIGMA PHI OR INVITATION TO LIFE FOR A DEPENDABLE ANSWER.

Each pledge training session should be about half an hour long.

Use the "Pledge Review" at the back of this book to make sure your pledges have fully understood their training. If 90% of your pledge class receives a grade of

80% or higher on the review, the pledge class is eligible for a special certificate of recognition from International. Write your division chairman at Beta sigma Phi International, P.O. Box 8500, Kansas City Missouri 64114-0500 for your Pledge Review Certificate of recognition.

When pledge training has been completed, plan a Ritual of Jewels ritual for your pledge class.

IMPORTANT FACTS TO REMEMBER

1. Pledges are eligible to serve as chapter officers, committee chairmen, and members of committees while they are pledges.

2. A pledge has full membership privileges upon joining.

3. A pledge has the same financial obligations to her local chapter and to the International organization as any other active member.

4. A pledge should be given some important responsibility immediately after she has received the Pledge ritual so that she may lend her ideas and make contributions to the chapter's success.

5. Regular pledge training meetings are a requirement.

6. A pledge serving as Vice-President of a new chapter does conduct pledge training.

BENEFITS OF MEMBERSHIP
• The Privilege of Transfer (we are in more than 10

countries with some 150,000 members)

- The Torch of Beta Sigma Phi, your monthly sorority magazine by subscription or online.
- Beta Sigma Phi Insurance Programs, for yourself and your family
- Scholarships, for yourself, your children, and your grandchildren
- Interest-free Medical Emergency Loan Fund
- Beta Sigma Phi cruises (great trips at great group rate!) and conventions
- Envoy program for Men Friends and Envoy 2 for young men
- Legacy Program (for daughters and other special girls)
- Beta Sigma Phi program outlines with hundreds of selections to choose from
- International Service Projects
- Contests for Individual Members and Chapters
- State and Provincial conventions
- The Beta sigma Phi Bed and Breakfast Program
- Yearly International Pen Pal Program
- Friendship with Sisters Around the World!

OUR MOTTO: Vita, Scientia, Amicitia
(Life, Learning, and Friendship)
OUR COLORS: Black and Gold
OUR FLOWER: The Yellow Rose
OUR FRUIT: Strawberry

First Meeting

INVITATION TO LIFE

RITUALS

1. THE PLEDGE RITUAL. One member should read the Pledge Ritual (see following pages) to the pledges and, through discussion, they should interpret it paragraph by paragraph. Too much emphasis cannot be given to a comprehensive understanding and to a sincere respect for our rituals. This should be an examination of the heart rather than of the mind. There is no time in life when the chapter members have a greater opportunity to show the initiate that Beta Sigma Phi is composed of "the friendliest, the loveliest-minded, and the most socially respected" women than at a Pledging ceremony.

2. THE OPENING RITUAL. At the opening of all meetings, all members stand in a circle, join hands, and repeat the following ritual:

"Sisters of Beta Sigma Phi, we pledge ourselves anew to the aims and purposes of our glorious sisterhood; more tolerance for our fellow beings through a better understanding of them; a clearer and deeper appreciation of the cultural and finer things of life for ourselves; and a determination to give the best that is in us to our sorority and to assist in any and every way to shed the light of our torch throughout the world."

3. THE CLOSING RITUAL. At the formal closing

of all meetings, all members stand in a circle and repeat the following ritual:

"Eternal Father, Shepherd of the Stars, guide us that we may follow only the Good, only the True, only the Beautiful. Hold aloft to us the guiding torch of wisdom and help us to push on, undaunted, toward its light. Illume our souls with Thy wisdom that we may light the way for those who follow us. If the road we take seems obscured in dust, give us skill and grace to pave it with stars, to transmute the dust into stardust. Grant us such clearness of vision, such sweetness of sprit, such earnestness of purpose, that we may follow the torch to our goal."

Members then join hands and repeat together:

"May the Lord watch between me and thee, while we are absent one from the other."

Pledges will be expected to know the Opening and Closing Rituals by heart before the end of pledge training. Practice at this meeting!

Questions for First Meeting

1. Briefly state any thought or thoughts from the Pledge Ritual which appealed to you.

2. What is the significance of the symbols on your Pledge Pin?

3. The fellowship of Beta Sigma Phi and its first greatest lesson is _____.

4. State thoughts from the Opening and Closing Rituals which particularly appeal to you.

PLEASE NOTE: The chapter president should be invited to the next pledge training meeting to explain the chapter yardstick and how each member is important in maintaining a good chapter rating. You should show the chapters copy of the previous year's yardstick and the achievements gained towards the current year's rating

In new chapters where no previous year's yardstick is available, the president should bring a copy of the yardstick (found in the March-April Torch provided in the chapter box of supplies). Together the members should examine the yardstick and mark achievements to date.

The next meeting will deal with the subject of basic rules of Parliamentary Procedure, and the duties of your chapter officers. In an established chapter, your chapter officers should be present at the next meeting to read and discuss the duties of their offices.

Beta Sigma Phi Pledge Ritual

A long table is covered with a white cloth reaching to the floor. In the center is a black bowl filled with the flower of the sorority, yellow roses. The Book of Ritual lies in the center behind the flowers. On each side are candle holders filled with black candles, or white candles may be used. They are lighted before the candidates are admitted. Pins for each candidate and yellow candles for each candidate are placed on the table in small separate trays

The President stands behind the table with any honorary members or international representatives on either side.

The members, standing in two rows the width of the Ritual table apart, are facing each other.

Candidates are in formal or dressy dress. If possible, candidates should not be permitted to see or enter the Ritual room until conducted in for the ceremony. The Vice President and Treasurer, or any two appointees, alternately attend the door, admitting and conducting candidates one or two at a time, to the Ritual table and from there to the correct place in the semi-circle being formed inside the two rows of members. Soft music may be played while the candidates are being conducted into the room.

The Director and Sponsor are conducted to the ritual table first and, after they have been formally admitted, are led to the chairs at the front corners of the table, and seated facing towards each other slightly and into the circle that is to be formed by members and candidates.

Before admittance of the candidates, the President speaks: "Who seeks admittance to Beta Sigma Phi?"

Door attendant replies, "Friends we have invited to join us."

The President, "Let them enter." The candidates are then brought into the room and stationed before the Ritual table. The attendant remains standing just a step back of the candidates.

Pledge Ritual

Please note: Asterisks have been inserted to suggest places to pause for breath. By practicing, you can determine which places are best for you.

*My friends we are here to explain to you * those things which will enable you to truly become a part * of the sisterhood of Beta Sigma Phi. ***

*Long ago, in the golden days of Greece, * a woman named Diotima was known * as the wise woman of Mantinea. * She was said to be the teacher of Socrates. * It was she who taught the great philosopher the meanings and importance of love. * She can serve as our guide also. * Through her we touch the spirit of immortal womanhood * which runs unbroken through all time. ***

*A story is told of a young woman * starting her search for wisdom. * She felt that she was wandering* *alone in the dark, * but found that she was not alone. * Diotima was with her, * guiding her and teaching her. * This is her story.*

As they walked together, * the young woman saw a light moving ahead of them. * She saw that it was a torch, * and they were following it.

"What is the torch?" she asked the wise woman. *

"It is called Learning," she answered. *

"Why does it move ahead as we move towards it?" *

"So you and I may find our way through the darkness." *

"But where does it lead," she persisted. * Diotima did not answer. *

"Where was the torch lighted?" she asked Diotima.

The answer came slow and measured. * "The torch was Lighted from a great fire. * Some call it Truth. * Some call it Beauty. * Some call it Love. * Those who follow it will learn all of these." *

"Will we reach the flame?" *

"You will enter its light, * but will never touch the flame. * The immortal spirit of womanhood is in every mortal woman. * It is part of her self. * But the ideal of Truth, Beauty, and Love * which are represented by the flame * are always beyond the individual. *

"Why are those we meet not also following the torch * and seeking the light, * instead wandering about in different ways?" *

"Because they cannot see the light. * They do not have the torch * such as I now give to you, * because

you have been found worthy." * And so Diotima handed to her the torch, * just as I hand it on to you. *

Follow the light of learning, * it will guide you well. *
Though your heart may become faint * and your foot-
steps may falter, * keep moving forward. * Patience
overcomes all things * but emotions can mislead us. *
Their ways are clouded by sensation. *

Know that you have a right to be useful. * To be a
Beta Sigma Phi * is to be worthy to follow the light of
the torch. * You must bear within you * the spirit of
immortal womanhood * of which the torch is a symbol. * You shall be kind, helpful, and friendly * to your
fellow beings. *

You shall be steadfast and faithful * in the pursuit
of the high ideal. * You shall give the best that is in you
to your work, * your life, * and to your world. * To be
a Beta Sigma Phi is to renounce selfishness * and to
assume a queenly quest. *

The fellowship of Beta Sigma Phi, * and the first
great lesson of its sisterhood * is love. * It is love which
springs between women * united by the same great
ideals. * During the weeks ahead * there shall be lighted from this torch * six others, six great perfections of
your inner self, * six ways of love. * Our love shall be
not only for living creatures, * but that all-embracing
love * for souls we never saw. * Their messages have
come down to us * in works of art, music and archi-
tecture. * In sculpture, books, pictures * and dance we
meet them. * All the avenues of beauty and glory *

to which we may open our hearts * and our minds in gratitude and growth. *

That love shall embrace ideas as well as persons. * It shall embrace both the heart * and the mind through constructive action and service. *

That love shall make us slow to expose a fault * and eager to find and to believe * the good and the true. * It shall cause us to share * in whatever good or sorrow * may come to any one of us. *

That love imparts to the body * and to the spirit * the full beauty and perfection * of which they are capable. *

And it crowns a woman in her queenly quest, * enriching most who gives most. *

The purpose of this fellowship shall be * to advance each one of us in the understanding * of the good and the true and the beautiful, * through appreciation of the arts, * and to enable each one of us * to make of her own life, * both in thought and conduct, * a work of art, * a masterpiece of beauty. *

Candidates for admission into Beta sigma Phi * are you willing to carry this torch. * If so, answer I am. *

Do you pledge yourselves to seek and follow the light of learning? * If so, answer, I do. *

Then repeat after me these words * "I solemnly promise to uphold * the honor and the aims * of Beta Sigma Phi * as I know them." *

I now inform you of the significance of this badge. * The great Phi is the golden circle of friendship. * We are bound in a union of unbroken strength. * Beta signifies life,* the gleam of time between two eternities. * The shaping of our own lives is our work. * It is a thing of beauty, a thing of shame * as we ourselves make it. *

The Sigma signifies learning. * It is wealth to the poor, * honor to the rich, * aid to the young, * support and comfort to the aged. * Learning, if rightly applied, * makes a woman cheerful and useful. * It is an ornament in prosperity, * a refuge in adversity, * and an entertainment at all times. * It cheers in solitude * and gives moderation and wisdom. *

The Beta and Sigma rest on a background of black, * signifying the death of selfishness, * for in loyal and loving service to others, * selfishness is forgotten. * The flaming torch is the light of learning, * a guide, * meaning that you are guided by the light of learning * and are yourself a guide to others. * She who seeks more light will always find it * and she is one of the happy few mortals in every point of time. * .

The yellow rose is the flower of this organization, * signifying in its purity and freshness * the wholesomeness of our undertaking. *

The torch is repeated in the great crest. * Here too is an ancient lamp of knowledge * and a book signifying the intellectual * and literary attributes * of our organization. * The Latin motto, * Vita, Scientia, Amicitia, * represent the purpose of our organization, * life, learning, and friendship. * Wherever you see this badge * or this crest, * know that the wearer is your sister. *

The test for membership * is one member whispering the words beta Sigma Phi. * If the wearer is a sister, * the answer will be * I am your sister. * The hand clasp shall follow.*

At the Ritual table, officiate shows handclasp by giving it to the assistant.

Now that you know the ideals of our sisterhood, * is it still your desire * to participate in Beta sigma Phi. If so, answer it is. *

This badge, the emblem of our sisterhood, * is placed upon you now. * Let no shame, no taint of any kind, * come upon it. * Treasure it and wear it with constancy. *

Attendants collect the candles, pin the badges, and give the handclasp with the test for membership.

I now pronounce you a pledge * of (insert chapter name here) chapter of Beta Sigma Phi. * Do not forget your promise.

UNDERSTANDING OUR RITUALS

To trace the origin and growth of ritual in Beta Sigma Phi is to draw the picture of the heart of an association of people devoted to the development of a better self as individuals, and to a better world.

Even the computer cannot turnout results that are good unless the right data is programmed into it. Rituals are programming by which Beta Sigma Phi feeds into the minds and hearts of its members the basic data from which they will, in time, be rewarded. The rewards are individual and personal results, differing in form but not in the essence from symbolic statements more general and abstract.

The urgency and variety of lesser things press upon us many hours of every day. But constructive thinking, to be most effective, must be habitual. It needs cultivation as a habit, until it is firmly established as one. Hence again, the rituals are of value – especially the ones repeated at every meeting. By repetition, we deepen our comprehension, and at the same time form a habit of good thought.

Beta Sigma Phi rituals are symbolic representations of the spirit of sisterhood and of the determination of the members to improve themselves and, in this way, make a better world. The language of the rituals is purposefully poetic, because of the heightened emotional impact made possible by that form of expression. It deals with images and stories outside our normal terms of reference, so the ideals and ideas expressed may be approached and appreciated, as if seen for the first time. In this way, the words themselves, and the things of which they are symbolic, are not the "old friend" and symbols of our school days, but the living, acting, effective ones by which we mature into valuable adults.

The very first ritual of Beta Sigma Phi, the Pledge Ritual, begins with a story which, like the ancient myths, imparts a message in a vivid way. The story concerns Diotima, the wise woman of Mantinea. To some experts, Diotima is a mythical person; others feel she did exist. She was reputed to be the teacher of Socrates, and a prophetess who taught that philosopher about the art and mystery of love. In Diotima's time, the idea that love as something more than physical desire was unheard of. Diotima taught that love is the very core of progress; the urge, the whip that drives us all toward projection of self and the creation of goodness, truth and beauty, which she maintained with the most sublime goals.

In the story in the Pledge Ritual, a woman slept and dreamed that she wandered in the night through quiet streets of an ancient city, in the company of Diotima. She saw the light and realized that it was a torch moving in the distance, she discovered they were following the torch. She asked Diotima what the torch was and was told it is called learning, and that it moved away through the darkness to show them the way. She dis-

covered that the torch never stopped, but always let on-
ward. Diotima told her that the torch itself was lighted
from a fire that some call truth, some call beauty, and
some called love; and that those who follow it learn all
of these. The symbolic message of the story is that each
new member of Beta Sigma Phi is handed a torch which
can guide her through her search for the good, the true,
and the beautiful.

The rest of the ritual expands on the opportunities
offered a new member through her acceptance of the
sisterhood of Beta Sigma Phi. It expands also on the
importance, depth and meaning of the Fellowship of
Beta Sigma Phi; and is a lesson of love that grows between women who have been "United at the same distaff." The word distaff is described as part of a spinning
wheel which has since Old English times symbolized
women, their work and concerns. And the ritual de-
scribes the scope and impact of that kind of love, that
kind of fellowship.

The second ritual of Beta Sigma Phi the Ritual of
Jewels, is chiefly concerned with beauty and with six
virtues.

These virtues are part of beauty, and shine forth from
you as though your life were a Crystal prism, separating
the light of the torch into the spectrum. The virtues are
courage, vision, humility, loyalty, fellowship and service.
The first three are represented by the colors red, yellow,
and blue, which are primary colors, and which signify
the importance of those three virtues. The last three

colors are secondary colors, each of which is formed by the combination of two primary colors, signifying that these virtues are seen as combinations of the virtues of courage, vision and humility.

The Exemplar Ritual is basically a recognition and an honor for those who proved themselves in Beta Sigma Phi. It reminds members of the basic principles, of the symbolism, and of what they have learned in practicing the principles themselves. It celebrates what they have learned, and what they have been together. It confers upon them the right to be known as one who exemplifies the highest purposes of Beta Sigma Phi, an Exemplar.

The Preceptor Ritual is, again, a ritual of honor. Its candidates are honored as examples of friendship and living examples of the precepts of the organization, which they not only exemplify, but teach. They are called upon to give special concentration each year to one of the six virtues.

The fifth ritual for the Laureate degree gives each member a symbol of honor, the laurel wreath. The laureates are urged to accept the continuing responsibility of progress and achievements. The Master Degree, our sixth ritual, is the penultimate degree, while Torchbearer, the seventh ritual, is the highest degree.

Each ritual becomes progressively simpler because more is already known, much has already been practiced, and a great deal has been achieved. Each ritual marks personal growth and group achievement.

Second meeting

INVITATION TO LIFE

CHAPTER PROCEDURE.
Reference: *The Book of Beta Sigma Phi*

Read and discuss the basic rules of Parliamentary Procedure in the *Book of Beta Sigma Phi*. Newly organized chapters should adopt a Parliamentary Authority to meet any such needs not covered in the procedures outlined in the *Book of Beta Sigma Phi*. In an established chapter, the pledges should learn what parliamentary Authority is used by the chapter. It is important that every member know good Parliamentary Procedure and this discussion should include ample training for making, amending, and voting on motions and the ways and means of introducing chapter business.

Each chapter of Beta Sigma Phi elects a president, vice-president, recording secretary, corresponding secretary, treasurer, and extension officer to compose of the chapter's Executive Board. The duties of the chapter officers can be found in the *Book of Beta Sigma Phi*. In an established chapter, the chapter's officers should be present to explain their duties. In a new chapter, the new officers should read their duties from the Book of Beta Sigma Phi and discuss them with the rest of the chapter.

The third meeting will deal with the Standing Committees and their functions. The chairmen of your chapter's Standing committees should be present at the next meeting to read and discuss their duties.

Questions for Second Meeting

1. Using the index in the Book of Beta Sigma Phi, to find the information, pledges in turn should be asked to read verbatim the answers to the following questions.

2. When do chapter elections take place?

3. Name the officers a chapter should elect.

4. If any officer moves away or becomes inactive how is the vacancy filled?

5. Who composes the Executive Board of the chapter?

6. On what matters does the Executive Board make decisions?

7. How may a decision of the Executive Board be changed?

8. Which officer generally leads the chapter in rushing?

9. Who mails the minutes of chapter meetings to International? When should minutes be mailed?

10. List four purposes of parliamentary procedure.

11. What is the proper motion if action is to be taken in regard to any committee report?

13. Explain the two kinds of motions?

14. What are the beginning words one uses when proposing a motion?

15. Can you change your vote? If so, when?

16. Review the duties of all officers.

EASY STEPS TO
MAKING A MOTION

1) Motion is made... "I move that..."

2) Seconded...

3) President states: "it has been moved and seconded that... (She states the motion)." "Is there any discussion?"

After discussion, if any, President states: "The motion is that... (states it again)...All in favor say 'aye'. Those opposed say 'no'." If the motion passes: The ayes have it and the motion is carried." If not" "The motion is dismissed."

CHAPTER MEETING AGENDA

"The meeting will please come to order. May we stand and repeat together the Opening Ritual."

"The Secretary will call the roll."

"The Secretary will read the minutes of the last meeting."

"Are there any corrections?"

(If not, "the minutes will stand approved as read.")

(If corrected, "The minutes are approved as corrected.")

"Is there any official communication from International?"

"Is there any other communication to be brought before the Chapter?"

(Invitations, thank yous, pamphlets/brochures received, etc.)

"Vice-President's report."

(Introduction of guests, report on rushing, transfers, etc.)

"May we have the Treasurer's report?

"Are there any corrections?"

If not, "The report will be placed on file subject to audit."

Note: "Any receipts? (Monies of any kind are submitted to the treasurer at this time.)

"Any bills?" (Anyone who has a bill to submit does so now. A motion is then made to pay all bills and treasurer writes checks."

"May we have the report of the Executive Board Meeting?"

(This is only a report, not the minutes... given by the recording secretary...if there is a recommendation and it needs chapter approval, a motion is made and recommendation is voted on now.)

"Are there reports from any other officer?"

"City Council report"

(Given by city council representative)

"Standing Committee reports"

Program -

Membership - (vice-president)

Social -

Publicity -

Ways & Means -

Service-

Other special committees -

"Is there any unfinished business?"

"Is there any new business?"

"Is there any further business to be brought up be-fore the meeting?"

(Passing the candles, etc.)

"The next meeting will be done on date, time, at place."

"The meeting is adjourned."

PLEDGE TRAINING DONE NOW IN A NEW CHAPTER. (15-30 minutes)

PROGRAM PRESENTED

"May we now stand and repeat together the Closing Ritual."

NOTES/THINGS TO CHECK ON:

QUESTIONS TO WRITE

DIRECTOR OF MEMBERSHIP: BETA SIGMA PHI INTERNATIONAL. 1800 West 91st Place, P.O. Box 8500, Kansas City, Missouri 64114 (816) 444-6800; 1-888-BETA-2-B-1; www.betasigmaphi.org.

QUESTIONS FOR ADVISER:

Dates-

Hostess

Co-Hostess

Absent-

THE EXECUTIVE BOARD

The Executive Board of the chapter, aside from the assigned duties of each officer, has the final responsibility for the chapter's success. This responsibility is theirs by virtue of their having been elected by their chapter to be the leaders in all the chapter's activities. The influence of the members of the Executive Board will extend into every phase of the organization's activities, so it is safe to say that the only point in common between the various members of the Executive Board in regard to their duties to the chapter is the area of leadership.

EACH OFFICER IS A LEADER

It is not the function of the Executive Board or any of its members to do the entire work of any part of the chapter activity. The President does not alone conduct a meeting. She is joined by her committee chairmen and other officers in presenting a well conducted and well organized meeting. The Vice President does not alone conduct the chapters rushing program, nor does any other officer dischargen her duties without assistance. Each officer is, in her own area, a leader. The President, by virtue of her general interest must be a leader in all areas. This requires the officers constituting the Executive Board, and particularly the president, to have a firm understanding of the principles of leadership. Without such an understanding, no amount of knowledge of the correct procedures, or even complete dedication to the goals of the chapter, will produce success.

LEADERSHIP IS NOT A MYSTERY

Leadership is not a mystery; it is not something with which we are endowed at birth that inspires others to follow us wherever we may lead. It is something which can be developed and which must be constantly practiced. There may be in the world intuitive leaders who can forge ahead, relying only on their own understanding of the goals, purposes and desires of those whom they lead. Much more certain of success are those leaders who ascertain, by the simple expedient of asking, what the aims and goals and desires of the group are. In Beta Sigma Phi, a very good way to accomplish this is through the use of a Member Interest Survey (see page 46, or on the Downloads page at www.betasigmaphi. org).

Many an officer has exercised diligently all the facets of leadership, except the all important one of knowing the direction in which she should be leading, only to find herself in the middle of her term separated from her members by a gulf of disinterest created by other interests.

LEADERSHIP IS A MATTER OF INSPIRATION

Once the goals, aims and directions of the chapter are understood, leadership becomes a matter of inspiration, guidance, and reward. If you are to be a leader, you must be ahead of those you are leading. From this position you cannot push them. How can you inspire them to accomplish the goals of the chapter? You can guide

them in their efforts so that the best methods and procedures are used – avoiding waste of time and wasted
effort. You can reward them by giving the recognition
and the praise their contributions deserve. The true
leader must accept the responsibility for failure, while
she may not accept all the credit for success. Why it
may seem unfair, this is entirely logical, because failure
is a result of a breakdown somewhere in the structure
of the chapter or committee, and a breakdown can be
corrected and many times avoided by a diligent leader.
Success is the result of combined effort when no breakdown has been allowed.

DEFFINITION OF EXCUTIVE

The duty of the Executive Board and each of its members is clearly implied in the definition of "executive".
An executive is one who executes or carries out the decisions that have been made by the group. It is the decision of the group that a meeting shall proceed smoothly, and therefore the President must conduct an orderly
meeting. The group decides that it wishes to have a certain number and certain kinds of social events, and the
Executive Board must arrange for a committee to carry
out these wishes of the group. The entire group obviously cannot be responsible for the chapter's funds, so
the Treasurer accepts the responsibility of executing
the chapter's wishes in regard to its money.

None of this must lead us to feel that every action
of the executive board and of each committee must be

approved in advance by the chapter. Certain of their actions must always be referred to the chapter, particularly in matters of spending money or matters of policy. To use the Vice-President as an example, she should plan the chapters rushing in cooperation with the chapter's Social Chairman. The general outline of the parties to be held should be formulated. It is not necessary for the entire chapter to take part in the preliminary planning. They will have their opportunity to change any part of the plans when the committees and officers make their reports at regular chapter meetings. If the plans are made at regular chapter meetings, great amounts of the chapter's time will be wasted. The same sort of thing is true for every other officer in the chapter.

PEAK OF RESPONSIBILITY

The peak of responsibility in the chapter rests with the President, since it is her responsibility not only to conduct the chapter meeting, but to oversee the general conduct of the affairs of the chapter. She must, with her Executive Board, appoint the committee chairmen and follow the activities of the committees to see if they function efficiently and properly.

She must also see that each of the officers on the Executive Board carries out her duties in the right way and in the right time. She will frequently need to serve as inspiration and a resource person for the other officers and committee chairmen to spark their thinking and to help them move in the way the chapter wishes them to go. In doing this, she must avoid the natural temptation to make all the decisions and to issue directives. She must also avoid the equally troublesome, but entirely opposite error of assigning responsibilities and then forgetting about them. Her lines of communication should be such that she knows what is under way in the work of each officer and committee and what the status of each project or interest is.

The President will need to call regular Executive Board meetings to dispose of chapter business that can be handled by the Executive Board, so that it may be reported to the chapter, but not actually handled, at the chapter meeting. She must occasionally meet with Standing and Special Committees, or with their chairmen, to see that the work of the committees is moving smoothly. She must be ready with suggestions for each officer and committee chairman to assist them in their work. She must be familiar with the yearly Calendar of Events so that planning and work can begin well in advance of any event or project. She should have constantly in mind the ideal chapter organization of officers and committees, and she should always use a basic agenda to plan each meeting of the chapter.

The Executive Board of the chapter should keep constantly in mind the basic purpose of Beta Sigma Phi. The chapter should be led in such a way that its concentration is always upon the basic purpose of the organization as they are stated in the following quotation from the International Constitution.

The OBJECT of this chapter shall be to unite congenially young women of the community for purposes of friendship and cultural development and for participation in the international sisterhood of Beta Sigma Phi.

Certainly, Beta Sigma Phi is a social organization. It is equally a cultural organization, and service has come to be a large part of Beta Sigma Phi. A chapter should undertake no project that does not in some way further the basic concerns of, and the basic purposes of, the chapter. There is, for instance, no reason why a service project cannot also be a social occasion, combining enjoyment and friendship with accomplishment.

RELATIONSHIP OF THE EXECUTIVE BOARD TO THE CHAPTER

To sum up the relationship of an Executive Board to the chapter, it is apparent that the Executive Board participates in two functions. With the committees, they are involved in preliminary planning. As an Executive Board alone, they make decisions that are necessary to carry out the chapter's wishes. As individual officers, they execute the chapter's wishes by virtue of performing the duties specifically designated to their offices. As leaders, they must seek the chapter's opinion and ask for its decision, rather than simply wait for the chapter to express an opinion or to reach a decision.

RESPONSIBILITY OF EXECUTIVE BOARD TO CITY COUNCIL

The executive board of the chapter also has a responsibility where a City Council exists to arrange the support of the chapters for the work of city council. Here again, the work of City Council is the work desired by the chapters and members, City Council does not have its own projects, City Council coordinates the projects of the chapters if they involve more than one chapter. This is the function of the City Council to work with the city-wide project in which all the chapters will be involved, and upon which all the chapters have decided. The function undertaken by City Council should not duplicate the functions of the chapters. It would not be necessary, for instance, for any city to have both City Council and chapter service projects. If a service project came up which required the work of more than one chapter and the chapters wish to undertake it, it would be coordinated by the City Council. City Council should not necessarily seek and accept service projects, and then elicit the support of the chapters.

If City Council is to work successfully in this way, the Executive Boards of the chapters must arrange for the necessary support for the projects which all the chapters in the city have decided to undertake. Through City Council representatives, they must keep the chapter informed of the progress of the projects, and they must arrange for their chapter to supply the necessary support in terms of time, effort and money. This means they will need to have a clear understanding of what time, effort and money are available from their chapter.

They must be able to find support in the chapter in the way of members to serve on committees, and to undertake special tasks to assure the success of projects coordinated by City Council. Only in this way can these projects be truly projects of the chapters. If the representatives to City Council must supply all the effort to projects, the projects are no longer projects of the chapters, but are City Council projects, and the City Council is functioning as a chapter.

In all that has gone before, we have been concerned with the Executive Board of the chapter. All the information applies equally to the Executive Board of City council. There are, in addition, certain specific things which vary a bit for the Executive board of City Council from the duties of a chapter Executive Board.

The President of City Council and the other officers and committee chairmen must be equally concerned to be certain of the direction and goals of all the members involved. In the case of City Council, this means all the members in the city. It places a special necessity on them for planning long in advance, since there are so many more people involved and the projects are normally so much larger. In all matters concerned with policy or the expenditures of large sums of money, enough time should be allowed for City Council representatives to receive definite instructions from their chapters. Special care must be taken in setting up committees and in following up their activities, because there arises usually a complication of greater difficulty in arranging City

Council committee meetings due to greater distances for the committee members to travel.

City Council executives must guard especially against creating rules and regulations for the chapters, and against making decisions which affect the internal operations of the chapters. City Council is similar to a parliamentary body, which may not make laws governing the internal operation of the cities, states, or provinces from which the representatives are elected.

COORDINATION IS A KEY WORD IN CITY COUNCIL ACTIVITY

This obviously imposes upon the City Council executives the necessity for the deepest possible understanding of the wishes and needs of the chapters and members who make up the Council. Information is available from the International Office which will assist City Councils also in undertaking an interest survey to assist them in planning their year. And planning an entire year in advance is just as important for a City council as it is for a chapter. It is remarkably difficult to have a successful year of activity with planning done on the spur of the moment or on a month to month basis. The Executive Board of the council must undertake to establish in advance what major social activities at least will be followed for the year. They must bear in mind the traditional activities that are carried on from year to year; they should outline the major social events, such as Founder's Day, rituals, and dances; they must determine what service projects the chapters wish to undertake on a city-wide basis and plan for those. In all of this, they must leave room so new activities may be fitted into the schedule.

The vision and imagination of the members of the Executive Board should be available to the chapter and to the Council. So also should their understanding and their friendship. The goal is to make the chapter or the Council fulfill as nearly as possible the social and cultural needs of every member and chapter. It is a worthy goal!

NOMINATION, ELCTION, AND INSTALLATION OF OFFICERS

Nominations shall be made from the floor at the second regular meeting in March each year. At this meeting, the President shall call for nominations from the floor, and nominations shall be made for each office-beginning with the President and proceeding through Vice-President, Recording Secretary, Corresponding Secretary, Treasurer, and Extension Officer. City Council representatives may also be elected at this same meeting.

Any active voting member is entitled to make a nomination.

A nomination does not need to be seconded.

No one member, except by general consent of the entire group, can nominate more than one member until after all members of the group have had the opportunity to nominate.

After nominations have been made, the President should ask, "Are there any further nominations? Hearing none, the nominations are closed." The nominations and voting for each office shall be complete before the nominations for the next office begin. A motion may be made to close the nominations. It must be passed by a two-thirds vote.

A vote shall be taken on each office in turn. The vote for each office shall be held immediately after the nominations for that office have been closed. The vote shall be by secret ballot and it shall require a majority of votes cast to elect.

Discussion of each candidate shall be limited to a three minute speech by the member placing that candidates' name in nomination. In the event only one nomination is made for any office, the vote for that office may be taken by voice or by show of hands.

When ballots are required, they shall be collected by two tellers appointed by the President. They will immediately count the ballots and write the results on a piece of paper, followed by their signatures, which shall immediately be given to the president. The President shall then announce the results of the ballot. In the event no candidate has received a majority, another ballot shall be taken. If there are more than two candidates, only the two having the largest number of votes on the first ballot shall be included for the second ballot.

At the conclusion of each balloting, the tellers will

place the ballots in envelopes, which shall be sealed and retained by the Secretary for 30 days.

In the event that any member feels there is an irregularity in any phase of the election, she shall make it know to the chapter immediately. The chapter may, at its discretion and upon a majority vote, declare the election for a specific office, or for the entire slate of officers, null and void if it finds there was an irregularity in the election procedures which would invalidate the election of any officer or of all officers.

Such an irregularity would be (1) a miscount of ballots; (2) nomination and election of a member ineligible by reason of inactivity upon the international roster; (3) leave of absence; or (4) member-at-large status locally. Failure to follow prescribed election procedures, if such failure could affect the outcome of the election, would also constitute an irregularity and of which election should be contested.

A ballot cast for anyone who has not been nominated shall be treated as a blank ballot; Ballots cast for an ineligible person shall be treated as a blank ballot.

Failure to contest the election before the meeting at which the election is held is adjourned, expresses tacit approval. No election may be contested at any time for any reason after the meeting at which the election held is adjourned.

If the procedures are followed, the election will be a true expression of the will of the majority of the chapter.

No matter how fine and capable she is, not every candidate can be elected. An election of officers is not a popularity contest; and so failure of a candidate to be elected should not under any circumstances be thought to reflect upon her or upon those who have nominated and supported her. To be nominated for office is a high honor. Candidates who have not been elected and those who have supported them should take the lead in offering congratulations and support to those who have been elected.

CHAPTER AND COUNCIL ELECTIONS

All too often in chapter or council elections, the vote becomes more of a popularity contest than a selection of the best candidates.

But when you get right down to the brass tacks, nominating a dear friend for an office for which she is not qualified is not an act of friendship. Your action may tell your friend you are proud of her and trust and rely upon her, but there are other and better ways to demonstrate your feelings. Every member of every chapter, and every representative to city council should give careful advance thought to those who will be nominated and to those for whom she will vote for each office. Some offices, such as the office of treasurer and recording secretary particularly, require special skills if they are to be handled in the best way and with the least amount of difficulty for the officer elected. Each office has some special requirement for which some members are better suited than others.

Every chapter or council is a bit different, but the general duties of each office are still very similar. Let's consider them.

What does it take to be a good president? A president needs to be well liked, but being the most popular member is not necessary. She needs much more to be steady, decisive, orderly, understanding, and above all, enthusiastic. She needs to understand the basis of the organization, its structure and its modes of operation. She needs to be well enough acquainted with the members of her chapter or council to understand their needs, desires, and wishes; she needs to be selfless enough to want those members desires fulfilled.

She needs to be able to keep track of the work of committees without interfering with it. She needs to be able to preside at a meeting without dominating it. It is her duty to execute the expressed wishes of the members, but not her duty to make all the plans and to do all the work herself. She is not someone upon who you dump all the projects and problems while you walk away and forget them. She is the leader, but not the ruler. No one will fill all those qualifications perfectly, but you should choose from among you the one who, at that time, can best fill those qualifications considering her own talents and available time.

The vice-president is not the understudy president. Simply presiding when the president is absent is not her chief duty. She leads the chapter, also, in a specific area.

She is the chapter's membership chairman. She is the rushing chairman and chapter hostess. She, too, needs great enthusiasm. She also needs a very good understanding of the organization so she can clearly and easily present it to prospective members. She needs to be gracious and interested in people so she can fulfill her role as hostess, and in city council do an effective job of helping transfers. Besides enthusiasm for the organization and chapter, she needs a clear understanding of membership needs in the chapter. In fact, she needs to know as much as anyone about Beta Sigma Phi, so she can give proper pledge training to the new members.

One of the most demanding jobs in any chapter is the job of the recording secretary. Ideally, the member elected to that position will have the mechanical skills, such as typing, which will make the position easy for her. A member who has to write down the minutes by hand and take copious notes in longhand is at a disadvantage. A recording secretary also needs to be an orderly, well-organized person. She should be good with details, and keep all the chapter and membership records, which are shared with International, up to date. She needs to be able to organize the notes she takes into clear, concise, and brief minutes and reports. She also needs the heartfelt thanks of every member for doing a difficult job.

The corresponding secretary needs to express the chapter's written communication graceful, clearly, and correctly. She needs to understand the proper forms of correspondence, such as formal and informal invitations, RSVPs, letters of condolence and congratulations, and business letters. Her job is lighter than the job of recording secretary, but very important. She is often the one who represents the chapter to people in the community. One of the really difficult jobs of the chapter or city council is the job of treasurer. It is amazing how often a member elected to the office of treasurer is not really good with numbers and has not experience with bookkeeping at all. It isn't unusual to hear a treasurer admit she has difficultly balancing her own checkbook. To elect such a member to the office of treasurer is almost mean. Treasurer's books for a Beta Sigma Phi chapter or city council should be as simple as possible. They should be kept clear, accurate, and up-to-date. The treasurer should have enough time to keep the books day-by-day rather than try to straighten them out every month or so. Her honesty goes without saying, but she should also be discreet, so that the financial affairs of the chapter and members of the chapter are kept confidential. Nothing can cause more unhappiness for a chapter or a member of your chapter than a treasurer without the talents required for this job

In a chapter, one of the most neglected offices is that of extension officer. Her chief duty, of course is to lead Friendly Venture projects undertaken by the chapter. Chapters often ignore the office because they do not intend to form a new chapter by Friendly Venture. However, the extension officer can have a tremendous effect in stabilizing the balance of chapters in a city by helping to form Ritual of Jewels chapters which will provide eligible candidates for the Exemplar chapter and other higher degree chapters in time. One or two enthusiastic, capable extension officers in a city can make a big difference. An extension officer's requirements are much the same as ones for vice-president; she will be even better off if she has a bit of special organizational talent, the ability to bring people together and help them move forward.

While they are not chapter officers, representatives of city council should be chosen very carefully. They not only need to be able to represent the chapter by being aware of the feelings and opinions and needs of the members of the chapter; they need the capacity to serve as officers and leaders of committees. No one should be sent as a representative to city council who would not be willing to serve in such a capacity and who, in the chapters opinion, does not have the ability to discharge the duties of a city council office.

The same general qualifications apply for city councils as for chapter. There is an additional consideration; that is, that all city council officers should be able to see the wide picture of Beta Sigma Phi in their city, and function not only as representatives of their chapters but as citywide leaders devoted to the best interests of the community of chapters and members.

For the sake of your own chapter, your council and

the individuals you will call upon to serve, think carefully before you cast your ballot.

INDIVIDUAL/EVERY
MEMBER
INTEREST SURVEY

This Chapter of Beta Sigma Phi is yours, to be part of and to meet your needs. All suggestions will be taken into consideration by the executive board when making plans for the chapter to be brought back for the chapter approval.

1. List your first, second and third program topic preference which you would prefer having as your program assignment - either to develop individuality or as part of a program team. The program topics are listed in the bulletin, Programs á la Carte.

1. _____
2. _____
3. _____

2. What type of cultural outings would you enjoy the most? List your first, second and third preferences.

1. _____
2. _____
3. _____

3. How many social activities a year do you think our chapter should have?

_____

4. List your first, second and third preferences as to the specific kinds of socials you suggest our chapter have sometime during the year.

1. _____
2. _____
3. _____

5. Do you think our chapter should have a money-making project this first year? If so, when? If so, list your first, second, and third preferences as to ways and means project(s) you personally would enjoy cooperating in during the coming year.

1. _____
2. _____
3. _____

6. Should our chapter plan to have any service projects during the coming year?

_____ YES _____ NO

7. If you feel that the chapter should sponsor one or

more service projects during the coming sorority year, please indicate the number of projects you feel should be sponsored.

_____

8. If you feel the chapter should have service project this first year, list the types of service projects you would help support in the coming year, both in time and effort.

1. _____
2. _____
3. _____

9. Would you prefer special rushing activities, or would you prefer to do individual rushing by having a member bring a guest to a regular meeting or activity so we can get acquainted?

_____ Prefer special rushing activities

_____ Prefer individual rushing at any time during the year

10. Bellow are listed the standing Committees of our chapter. Please indicate your first, second and third preferences for committee assignments.

_____ Program committee

_____ Ways and Means Committee

_____ Social Committee

_____ Service

_____ Membership

_____ Publicity

11. Indicate any other items of concern or special interest below (not required):

_____

_____

_____

_____

_____

_____

_____

_____

_____

_____

_____

_____

_____

_____

_____

_____

_____

Third Meeting

INVITATION TO LIFE

ALL ABOUT COMMITTEES

The following shall be the standing commitees of the chapter: Program, Membership, Social, Publicity, Ways and Means, and Service. The duties and functions of these committees can be found in the *Book of Beta Sigma Phi*. The chairman of each commitee should now read the duties of her committee and discuss them with the pledges. In a new chapter, the chairmen should read their duties from the *Book of Beta Sigma Phi*, and discuss them with the chapter members.

In addition to the Standing Committees, Special Committees may be appointed by the chapter president when necessary. These committees shall continue to exist until they have completed their appointed task or until dissolved by the president.

Questions for Third Meeting

1. What are the Standing Committees in a Beta Sigma Phi chapter?

2. How are they formed?

3. How long do they serve?

4. Why is a Special Committee formed?

5. How long does a Special Committee function?

6. When does a committee report to the chapter?

7. When should a pledge be appointed to a committee? When should committees meet?

8. Who takes the responsibility of overseeing committees?

TIPS FOR COMMITTEES

1. WHY HAVE A COMMITTEE? A committee is simply a smaller version of the chapter itself. An entire chapter is too large and unwieldy a number to be concerned in the preliminary planning of every detail of chapter activity. The preliminary planning, therefore, is delegated to a committee which is representative of the chapter, and which is able to function smoothly and efficiently because of its size and special interest in a particular activity or area of chapter or council business.

2. AN EFFCTIVE COMMITTEE: Effective committees will shorten the time of the business meetings because of the effect of the planning already accomplished.

a. The membership of a committee should represent the chapter membership as directly as possible.

b. The members of an effective committee are doers who want to think originally, rather than "rubber stamp" others' ideas.

c. The members of an effective committee maintain happy working relationships even though their individual viewpoints may differ.

3. WHAT MAKES A COMMITTEE FUNCTION SUCESSFULLY?

a. Having a chairman who is a good leader.

b. Recognition of the importance of each member on the committee.

c. Sincere, interested and eager members who are able to attend meetings and willing to find a common ground for her ideas and those of the other committee members make a committee successful.

d. Awareness that time and patience are required for good group discussion.

4. A GOOD CHAIRMAN AND COMMITTEE MEMBERS CAN WELD THEIR INDIVIDUAL IDEAS INTO A GROUP DECISION.

a. Chairman assumes leadership by 1) Creating an informational conversational atmosphere. 2) Steering the discussion toward the accomplishment of the goal without permitting her own ideas to dominate the discussion. 3) Being receptive to and appreciative of committee members' opinions. 4) Trying in the kindest possible manner to help those who may have a little difficulty expressing themselves. 5) Drawing out ideas from those who are timid or reluctant into express themselves.

b. Assumes responsibility for starting discussions: 1) she makes sure members have an understanding of the scope of the work to be undertaken. 2) She may outline or list the main points of the questions being considered and ask members to agree on what they consider the best approach for finding a solution to the question. 3) She may call for the discussion of alternate points of view or for additional information when the need for such is indicated.

c. She keeps the discussion moving along by: 1) encouraging individual members to speak. 2) Remaining neutral when disagreements develop on the discussion. 3) Turning back to the group questions directed at the chairman, giving the group the opportunity to answer them. 4) Presenting questions in such a way that their answers will bring out useful information or opinions rather than just a yes or a no reply. 5) Summarizing points of view offered by Individual members by:

• Occasionally summarizing the discussion so you can more easily move to a new point in the discussion.

• Bringing the discussion back to the main point from which it has strayed.

• Listing important points of agreement or disagreement. It is advisable to look first for the points on which there is agreement and then work out whatever remaining questions there are on which the group has not yet agreed.

d. Brings the discussion to a close by: 1) Finishing the points before the members lose interest. 2) Summarizing the main ideas expressed by the group. 3) Asking the group to verify these summaries. 4) Leading the group to taking action by asking for a motion or recommendation from the group. 5) Giving recognition and praise to the group for its accomplishments.

6) making sure all committee members are clear as to the time, place and subject of the next meeting before this one is adjourned.

COMMITTEE PLANNING AND ACTION

THE COMMITTEE INVESTIGATES:

a. It finds out what activities the chapter would like, either by questionnaire from each member or by pooling the ideas of the committee members, instead of by discussion at a chapter meeting. NOTE: Having all members at a chapter meeting enter into discussion of details is usually considered wasted time and effort and frequently results in nobody knowing what has actually been decided. If members wish to have some part of the committees' suggested plan changed, they should give their suggestions briefly. If the rest of the chapter agrees, the committee will look into the suggestion and report back.

b. It finds out what facilities in the community are open to the chapter. For example, social committee should keep up on what plays or special events are coming, or places to hold parties, etc.; service committee contacts welfare agencies to know where service is needed, or may contact civic agencies to see with what civic projects the chapter can help; ways and means committee keeps its eyes and ears open for money-raising project possibilities.

THE COMMITTEE PLANS:

In committee meeting, a suggested plan for coming activities is drawn up. This plan would not be detailed until approved by the chapter, and for the most part would give just: *Type of activity; Suggested place; Suggested Date* (approximate).

The schedule should be drawn up for a minimum of three months in advance, preferable for six months or even a year's calendar may be tentatively planned at one time.

THE COMMITTEE REPORTS:

The Chairman would report to the chapter something like this " The committee thought the chapter would like the following calendar of activities for the coming months" . . .outline your schedule. . ."we will be reporting to the chapter in detail, before the time for these activities, to let you know the exact time and other details, if you approve of these plans in general. If any members wish to make suggestions for entertainment, refreshments, etc. at any activity, the committee will welcome the suggestions."

Chapter then votes to approve the schedule or ask the committee to change any part of it, so that the committee can go ahead and make definite plans. Chapter should not hold long discussion about details. Instead, members' ideas may be briefly given to the committee to be worked out and later reported to the chapter.

THE COMMITTEE ACTS:

When it comes time to put the plans for special events into action, the committee may divide: one or two members to look after transportation; one or two to look after refreshments; others to plan entertainment, etc. In this phase of committee action or work, the chairman may ask for extra members to help. The Chairman should ask the President to appoint other members to help the committee temporarily. In some cases the whole chapter likes to work on the activity.

SAMPLE:
COMMITTEE PLANNING SHEET

EVENT: Annual Champagne brunch
THEME: "TOASTING RENAISSANCE"
DATE: Sunday, January 12
TIME: 11:30 a.m.
PLACE: Monica's
DRESS: up!

SPECIAL DISCUSSION ACTIVITY:

Finding Renaissance... revealing info about ourselves that others may not know or would find to be new, interesting, profound, shocking (!), unreal (!), unbelievable, etc... etc.

MENU:
  CHAMPANGE
  MIMOSAS
  COFFEE
  FRUIT SALAD
  WALDORF SALAD
  BAKED FRENCH TOAST
  CRABMEAT QUICHE
  CHERRIES JUBILEE (FLAMING)

WHO IN THE COMMITTEE WILL DO WHAT
  Cheryl R.- Waldorf salad
  Jane- purchase champagne (2 ½ cases), orange juice, strawberries
  Marilyn- quiches
  Merrilee- cherries jubilee, LARGE champagne classes for flaming jubilees
  Monica- baked French toast, coffee, 2 candlesticks, plates, cups for coffee, syrup, powdered sugar
  Sherryl C - Fruit salad, plates, discussion sheets, pens/pencils

NEEDED:
  Card table/chairs
  Silverware
  White tablecloths

YEARBOOK

The chapter yearbook is a very helpful and useful resource that every member will enjoy. All members will refer to it often...

WHAT IS THE YEARBOOK?

Yearbooks include planning for stimulation of interest and participation in programs, socials, service, ways and means, a roster of members' names, committees, officers; also, a calendar of chapter activities.

WHEN IS THE YEARBOOK PUT TOGETHER?

During the summer. Each member is presented with her own yearbook on Beginning Day. Actually, that is what Beginning Day (last Sunday in August) is all about! A rally day, so to speak, to learn about what is planned and get ENTHUSIASTIC about the upcoming year ahead. Each committee chairperson outlines briefly what the committees have planned in regards to year activities tentatively scheduled for the coming year. The chapter votes, at the conclusion of all reports, to accept the contents... (Or recommends the committee make adjustments, etc.) One member put it this way – "THE YEARBOOK IS THE SIZZLING BEST SELLER OF BETA SIGMA PHI! IF YOU WANT TO KNOW WHERE, WHEN, AND WHO, THEN THIS IS YOUR COMMITTEE. BE IN THE KNOW! BE THE FIRST TO KNOW! ALL THE WORK TO

PUT THIS VALUABLE REFERENCE TOGETHER
IS DONE IN THE SUMMER—THE REST OF THE
YEAR IS SPENT READING IT!"

WHAT IS THE ADVANTAGE OF HAVING A YEARBOOK? HOW WILL IT HELP?

First of all, everything is together IN ONE PLACE!
The entire sorority year is planned in advance and this
saves time during the rest of the year. Keep in mind
that events and activities planned are tentative. Finishing details are added via committees as you go along.
Remember that FLEXIBILITY is a key Beta Sigma Phi
word… you do have the option to change your plans
or reschedule your events midstream. The tremendous advantage is that you know in advance the events
planned, meetings schedules, the date you are to give
your program, be a hostess or co-hostess and you can
then plan and prepare accordingly. Plus, you don't have
to waste precious meeting time to plan your upcoming activities. ALL PLANNING IS TO BE DONE IN
COMMITTEE, ONLY REPORTED AT THE MEET-
INGS! THIS WILL PROVIDE A SHORTER BUSI-
NESS MEEDTING AND MORE TIME FOR YOUR
PROGRAM AND SOCIALIZING!

WHAT ABOUT COVERS FOR THE YEAR-BOOKS?

The covers can be whatever you want…the sky's the
limit! Most chapters use a binder notebook of various

descriptions. Some are small to fit in your purse, others are 8 ½ by 11 size. It is up to the yearbook committee to decide what the covers will be. They appreciate your suggestions and ideas! Some chapters have each member create their own yearbook cover. Keep it simple and enjoyable, concentrating on the contents!

HOW DO WE GO ABOUT OBTAINING INFORMATION FOR THE YEARBOOK?

1. A COMMITTEE OF 2 OR 4 CAN BE APPOINTED (OR VONUNTEER) TO BE ON IT. It is helpful if someone who has access to a computer, printer or copier. Saves time and $$$!

2. Conduct an individual/every member survey.

3. Have members 'sign-up' for hostessing, co-hostessing meetings, giving programs.

4. Distribute ideas from survey to committee chairpersons (social, ways and means, service, etc.).

5. Committees meet... One meeting during the summer is all that is necessary; this meeting is informal with the express purpose of planning that committees' activities for the coming sorority year. Activities are planned starting with the Beginning day (in August) Through the end of May. For example, the social committee would plan a social for September something like this:

SEPTEMBER SOCIAL
Event: Tailgate Party
Date: Sat. September 27th
Place: Lot 7 next to the UW Football stadium
(Regent Street)
Time: 11:00 a.m.
Dress: get the red out
Couple's Social

The above information would be what is tentatively planned by the social committee during the summer. Details from the social committee are given at the September meeting prior to the social.

6. After the committees meet and decide their activities, a tentative budget is made and submitted to the executive board.

7. Executive board meets with committee chairpersons and formulates the chapter's budget. The budget is approved by all members of the chapter on Beginning Day.

8. The yearbook committee sets a deadline of when all the above information should be submitted. Allow plenty of time to type and make copies. Remember to make EXTRAS for new pledges you will be adding to your chapter membership.

9. Coordinate plans for making covers.

10. Distribute yearbooks on Beginning Day. Your work is done!

11. Consider an electronic yearbook.

BASIC OUTLINE FOR
A GOOD CHAPTER YEARBOOK

- Opening Ritual
- List of Committees (if assigned)
- Chapter Roster (name and phone numbers only of each member)
- Meeting Schedule
    - Date:
    - Time:
    - Hostess:
    - Co-Hostess:
    - Program:
      - By Whom:
- Social and Cultural events (can be incorporated in Meeting Schedule)
- Budget (if one adopted)
- Individual member page with pertinent data and directions to home
- Closing Ritual

Yearbooks can include much more information than this basic package. Your chapter may also wish to include a letter from the chapter president that discusses chapter goals; chapter history; bylaws, rules and traditions; calendars and more. Ask International for further information on yearbooks.

Fourth Meeting

INVITATION TO LIFE

PROGRAMS

Nothing in Beta Sigma Phi is more important than our cultural programs, because they are the basic element of our organization. Programs permit and encourage each member to grow. Programs are designed to broaden your knowledge and understanding of yourself, your friends, and the world.

Our programs are basically humanity studies in the area of liberal arts. Each program should consist of a presentation and a discussion period. The presentation itself may be a lecture, a panel discussion, an audio visual event, a visit to a museum, or a cultural event. A guest speaker will occasionally enliven the program year, but most programs are presented by the members themselves. Chapters vary in their approaches to program assignments; usually when a chapter is new, pledges are "teamed up" so they can work together to prepare a program. However, as members get more comfortable with the idea of program presentations, they can certainly do them by themselves if that is desirable.

There should be a Beta Sigma Phi program at ever meeting during the year. Members are encouraged to use our "Programs á la Carte" program outlines, which are shared in the March-April issue of The Torch each year, and available year-round at www.betasigmaphi.

org under "Proram Outlines." Each of the 150 program outlines are designed to stimulate thinking, and help the members prepare the program. It is not necessary to present each program exactly the way it is outlined. If the interests of the members of a chapter or those members presenting the programs, lean in a slightly different direction, so much better. The better the program is adapted to the special interests and desires of the members of each chapter, the more successful it will be in accomplishing its purposes.

To make a program excellent, good preparation is a must. The program outlines will give you references and your local library and librarian will be invaluable in helping you find resources for your program.

HOW TO PREPARE FOR YOUR PROGRAM

Begin early. Give yourself plenty of time to become familiar with your subject. The local library has encyclopedias, current magazines, newspaper, and audio-visual materials that can enhance your subject presentation.

Dress up your program title if you wish. An intriguing title is like bait on a hook! It is your first chance to catch your audience's interest. Try to gain member's interest immediately in your talk by means of a quotation, a human interest story, or a means for arousing their curiosity.

Use good illustrative material – pictures, slides, displays, art objects, recordings, etc.

Practice your program until you can talk about it easily and do not have to read your notes. An informal approach will make your talk much more interesting to your audience.

Make the closing of your talk effective by summarizing your main points and finishing off with a rousing last few lines- perhaps a good quotation of a few lines of poetry.

Remember that the outlines provided in the program books are only outlines. There are an infinite number of ways to adapt and present the materials suggested in the outline. Programs should be about 30 minutes in duration.

Questions for Fourth Meeting

1. How much time should be devoted to the cultural program part of the meeting?

2. How are program assignments made in your chapter?

3. The programs are done in outline form. Should you adhere strictly to the outline?

4. How many cultural program meetings should your chapter have in a sorority year?

EFFECTIVE PUBLIC SPEAKING
By Mary Malins

In our professional lives and our personal lives, we are often called upon to make a presentation. Of course, this is a skill we can develop in sorority, since we all must research, organize and present programs in our chapter meetings. However, even speaking in front of a supportive group of sorority sisters can be a nerve-wraking, frightening experience! There are several steps you can take to dispel the fear of public speaking, and turn it into a pleasurable experience for all concerned.

Usually, we are asked to speak on subjects about which we already have some knowledge. If you can choose the subject, choose one you are enthusiastic about. Think about speakers you have enjoyed, and try to remember what it was that made their presentations memorable.

It is also essential that you know the subject you will be discussing. You must do the research, reading or interviewing to collect the necessary background information. Allow yourself adequate time to do this. Even if your talk is on a subject you know well, review and update your knowledge. There is nothing more annoying or insulting to an audience than a speaker who, obviously unprepared, begins to "wing it".

Another important aspect of public speaking is that of organization. Everyone can recall listening to a speaker who goes off on so many tangents that he is difficult to follow. Be very clear with your audience about what you will present; then present it, sticking to your main points or outline. Review those same points in your summary. Be certain additional information you present emphasizes and reiterates those points.

You should write out your comments and practice, practice, practice! If you do this, you will be able to talk with very few notes, and give your speech with just an occasional glance at your outline. Use a friend or your mirror to help you practice. Here are a few more hints:

Keep well within the time you are allowed, and do not go over that time allotment. By sticking to your format, you show respect for your audience's gift to you of their time and attention.

Develop a real awareness of your audience. First, know who these people are and what their interests are; second, pay attention to their response to you during your talk. If they seem to be fidgeting, looking at their watches or studying the clock, you better take note! Ask a question, or tell a story; do something to keep their interest up! Check your time, and consider shortening the talk.

Speak appropriately. Do not use obscure words or acronyms unless you are certain your audience will understand them.

If you follow these pointers, you can have a great time giving a talk. By preparing your information, yourself, and your presentation, you can share, with your audi-

ence, a rewarding experience.
Fifth Meeting

INVITATION TO LIFE

DEGREES AND REQUIREMENTS

There are seven degrees in Beta Sigma Phi. They are Nu Phi Mu, Ritual of Jewels, Exemplar, Preceptor, Laureate, Master, and Torchbearer. The degrees are arranged to provide logical progression for a member as she grows in knowledge of the organization and in chapter cultural experience. As a member qualifies for each degree, she progresses from one degree to another.

The first degree is the Nu Phi Mu degree, where members from 18 to 22 years of age generally join the organization. Each member joins as a pledge, and after six months may qualify for her second ritual. In the Nu Phi Mu degree that ritual is the Ritual of the Badge.

When a Nu Phi Mu member has completed three years of program study and membership participation, she is eligible for progression to the Ritual of Jewels degree. Members may also join as brand-new members in the Ritual of Jewels degree chapters and are pledges for the first six months. At that time, they may qualify for the Ritual of Jewels degree. Members advancing from Nu Phi Mu degree receive the Ritual of Jewels degree immediately and do not go through pledge training again.

When a Member has completed four years in the Ritual of Jewels chapter, she becomes eligible to progress to the Exemplar chapter. Most members come to the Exemplar chapter by progression. It is, however, possible for a brand-new member to join an Exemplar, Preceptor, Laureate, Master or Torchbearer chapter. They have a pledge period followed by the Ritual of Jewels degree. After four years they receive the Exemplar Degree. After six years as exemplar members, they are eligible for the next higher degree, which is the Preceptor degree. After completing eight years of program work in the Preceptor degree, a member becomes eligible for the Laureate degree. Members who complete ten years of program work in the Laureate degree then become eligible for the Master degree. After 12 years of holding the Master degree, they are eligible for the Torchbearer degree, sorority's seventh and highest degree.

In most cases, the members will come to a higher degree chapter from more than one chapter of the lower degree. This serves to further strengthen the expanding quality of the friendships which are formed as a member rises in the organization. Members may receive a higher degree in a lower degree chapter when they become eligible.

WHY WE PROGRESS

Progression in Beta Sigma Phi provides opportunities for members to grow in stature, spirit, achievement, and abilities. Progression gives the members who move up in degrees an opportunity to face some new challenges, and widen their circle of friendship. It gives members remaining in the lower degree chapter an opportunity to take on leadership roles in the chapter.

A chapter does not vote on progressing members.

The names of the seven degrees of Beta Sigma Phi are derived from the Rituals of each degree. The organization itself, however, and each chapter in the organization, is named with letters from the Greek alphabet. The letters Beta Sigma Phi are the first letters of the Greek words meaning life, learning and friendship. The words represented by those letters are Bios, Sophia, and Philos. Chapters of Beta Sigma Phi derive their names from the Greek Alphabet, but with no particular meaning attached to the letters. They are assigned in alphabetical order.

The Greek alphabet is reproduced in this book, along with the proper pronunciation of each letter. You do not need to memorize the alphabet, but you will want to be familiar with it so that you can easily pronounce the names of the chapters in your own area, and recognize the Greek letter symbols.

The sixth meeting discusses membership status. Be prepared to discuss these statuses before the next meeting.

Questions for Fifth Meeting

1. How many Degrees are there in Beta Sigma Phi? What are their colors?

2. Name each degree in order from the first possible degree to the highest degree.

3. Is a member's age related to her degree?

4. What is the requirement to progress from your present degree to the highest degree?

5. What is the requirement to progress form your present degree to the next higher degree?

6. Write the Greek letter symbols for your chapter name.

7. How many degrees of chapters are represented in your town?

8. Does a chapter vote on members progressing?

Sixth Meeting

INVITATION TO LIFE

MEMBERSHIP STATUS

There are only a few kinds of membership Status in Beta Sigma Phi. Once you have become acquainted with them, you find that they are designed to provide for members exactly the kind of status they need at the moment. Here are the details of each membership status in the organization.

1. ACTIVE MEMBERS. Refers to members paying annual fees in the International organization and in good standing. Three kinds of active status are:

a. Active participation in a chapter

b. Leave-of-absence. A member who is on leave-of-absence is an active member in the International organization and she is an active member in her chapter. She is, however excused from attendance at chapter meetings for a period of up to one year.

A leave-of-absence is granted by the chapter for a specific period of time at the request of the member. At the end of that time the member returns to active participation in the chapter. If the member requires more than one year of less than full, active membership in the chapter, she must take a member-at-large status. (There is a special status for member with long-term illnesses; contact International for information on this status).

c. Member-at-large. A member-at-large is an active

member in the International organization and has no chapter affiliation. She may attend chapter meetings, socials or other Beta Sigma Phi events, by invitation. She has no responsibility to any specific chapter. The member at large status is granted by the International Office and the member on this status pays annual fees, just as any other active member does. She may apply for transfer to any chapter in the organization. Member-at-large time may be worked off through individual program work.

2. INACTIVE MEMBERS. The other main status of membership is inactive. On the inactive status a member does not pay annual fees and of course has no chapter affiliation or privileges. A member who has taken an Inactive status may become active again by reinstating her membership. She can be reinstated by a two-thirds vote of a chapter and by paying the reinstatement fee to International. This term needs special understanding. It refers only to members who are not active in the International organization. Active members who are not actively participating in a chapter are not referred to as inactive members, but as members on leave-of-absence or member-at-large.

3. HONORARY MEMBERS. There are also Honorary members in Beta Sigma Phi. A chapter may, if it wishes to, have a Director, Sponsor, or a chapter Honorary Member. A City Council may also recommend to the international Executive Council a woman who is known nationally and internationally for her outstand-

ing achievements to be considered for International Honorary Membership. No Honorary member of Beta Sigma Phi, whether Sponsor, Director, Honorary member or International Honorary Member, may be an active or inactive member of Beta Sigma Phi. Honorary Members are chosen from outside the organization for their special achievements, talents, and their interest in Beta Sigma Phi and the chapter or City Council. Honorary members to not pay chapter dues or assessments and also do not pay International fees. Your division chairman can give you information on appointment and installation.

a. Director. A Director is an Honorary Member chosen by a chapter to serve as a consultant on cultural programs for a limited period of one year. A woman possessing high qualities of leadership and intellectual interest should be chosen. A Director may be reappointed each year as long as it is mutually agreeable to the director and to the chapter.

b. Sponsor. A Sponsor may be named by the chapter for a period of one year to work in cooperation with the Social committee to assist with the chapter's social standing in the community. A sponsor may be reappointed each year as long as it is mutually agreeable with the Sponsor and the chapter.

c. Chapter Honorary member. An outstanding woman of the community who may give service of particular value to the chapter may be named by the chapter as Honorary Member. A Chapter Honorary Member may be reappointed each year as long as it is mutually agreeable with the Honorary Member and the chapter.

SPECIAL NOTE: The distinction made in some organizations between pledge members and active members does not exist in Beta Sigma Phi. A pledge to Beta Sigma Phi is a full member as soon as she has received the pledge ritual. She has all the rights and privileges of membership from that point on.

At the next meeting, the history of beta sigma Phi will be studied. Please review the materials before that meeting.

Questions for the Sixth Meeting

1. What are the three statuses of active membership?

2. Chapters may have members of only two statues. What are they?

3. Define a member-at-large; member on leave-of-absence; inactive member; active member.

4. Who grants a leave-of-absence?

5. Who grants a member-at-large status?

6. What special interest does each of the following have in chapter activity: Director? Sponsor?

7. For how long are a Director, Sponsor, or Honorary member appointed?

8. If your chapter has a member who will be out of town for three or six months, or who for some other reason cannot attend meetings for that length of time, what membership status would she request?

9. Who should let the International Office know when there is any change in a member's status?

10. What are the privileges of the pledge?

11. Does a member on leave-of-absence pay her annual membership fee to International?

Seventh Meeting

INVITATION TO LIFE

Beta Sigma Phi is a unique organization – so it seems fitting that we began in a unique time in world history, the Depression. In 1931, Beta Sigma Phi was there to offer young women something for themselves which was creative and productive and hopeful during a time filled with economic despair. We began in this atmosphere, and our organization has been able to grow and change in answer to the changing needs of our members through the depression, inflation, recession, war and peace.

A young man with a dream decided to share his idea with the young women of Abilene, Kansas. Walter W. Ross had been selling encyclopedias to local parent-teacher organizations throughout the Midwest, and has met so many women who, because of the time and economic depression, had virtually no social outlets. He decided to offer them a series of programs of study. He first went to Abilene, Kansas, and stopped at the Sunflower Hotel. That was where the very first chapter of what was to become a worldwide organization was founded. He told his story to seven young women, sharing with them his ideas for what he had decided to call "The National What to Read Club." The idea must have been exciting to this audience, especially when you realize that several of the original members remained active in Beta Sigma Phi their whole lives! After the first chapter was organized, he took his dream to Vinita, Oklahoma. Walter W. Ross tells the story best:

"I drove my little car into Vinita, Oklahoma, on a day of overcast sky. It was a typical country town of 5,000 people and only a part of the main street was paved. There was a rather nice new hotel called the Vinita Hotel which had just opened. I went in and sat down a bit and then walked all over the whole town. I asked the hotel clerk if he had lived there long and he said he had lived there a long time. Then I asked him who was the most prominent woman in Vinita and he told me without question it was Mrs. Leona V. Schroers. I called her and she allowed me to come and see her. I explained to her my dream of Beta Sigma Phi (although I was then calling it 'The National What to Read Club' because I wanted to see if the program which we had was strong enough to succeed in the early stages without an attractive name.)

"I began to show her my papers and tell her the thoughts that I had about this young organization-to-be. After a while, she said to me: 'Young man, you have a wonderful idea, but you are a bit awkward in presenting it. Give me those papers and come back here at four o'clock this afternoon.' I did as I was told and when I went back she had twelve young women in her living room and right then and there we established a chapter of 'The National What to Read Club.'"

"I have visited them many times since then and the

first treasurer has told me that even though they gave small checks as first payments for their fees, she was in the bank and did not clear the checks until all of the supplies that I had promised them arrived. I thought that was a rather amazing sidelight.

"We had our installation dinner and we called in a local photographer to take a flash picture. He had an old-fashioned business that was just a tiny trough on a stick with powder in it and he touched the match to the powder and took the picture. Little did we know that night that that was the beginning of one of the greatest organizations our modern world has seen.

"The next day Mrs. Schroers told me to come by the house, which I did. 'Now,' she said, 'I want you to go down and see the greatest woman in Oklahoma, Mrs. Sally Rogers McSpadden, Will Roger's sister.'

"Mrs. McSpadden had raised Will Rogers and was in many ways was very much like him. Of course, I took Mrs. Schoers's advice and Mrs. McSpadden, who at the time was very active in the National Federation of Women's Clubs, gave me much help on program planning and the organization of chapters and was a guiding light to me personally during the rest of her life. She became our first International Honorary Member.

When Will Rogers was killed, The Torch of Beta Sigma Phi was the only periodical in the world that had an interview with the family. After leaving Mrs. McSpadden that first day, I went to the office and brought together the first steps in Beta Sigma Phi. We had adopted as a motto, 'Life, Learning, and friendship,' and we found that the three Greek words which mean life, learning, and friendship begin with the letters Beta, Sigma, and Phi, and so there we had the name of our new organization."

The Depression had a strange and wonderful effect on the growth of the organization. One of our first members recalls that she was earning $7.00 a week, and even such a small amount was good pay for the times. She couldn't have a vacation or go to the theater, and she felt she had very little to look forward to in life. She needed Beta Sigma Phi; she could not do without the things it offered; and for her, as for so many others, Beta Sigma Phi came at exactly the right time. (The membership fee and first year's annual fee, which at the time was $29.50, amounted to over a month's salary for her!)

The growth of Beta Sigma Phi from seven members in Abilene, Kansas to over 250,000 members throughout the world seems remarkable - but it did not surprise Mr. Ross. He believed in the dream, and expected the growth, and planned for it. But no one could have foreseen the spiritual growth and meaning Beta Sigma Phi has come to have in so many lives. Walter Ross said, "I am quite sure that all these things have come from the quality and character of the members themselves."

These statements contain the reason why Beta Sigma Phi has appealed equally to women all over the world. From the very earliest days, efforts were made to give the members what they themselves wanted, because then, as now, Beta Sigma Phi exists to serve its members. In February, 1932, the Educational Foundation was formed and incorporated to handle the financial affairs of the sorority. A few months later, in April of the same year, Beta Sigma Phi was incorporated under a charter granted by the state of Missouri. Today, Beta Sigma Phi is a non-profit corporation which maintains a contract with Walter W. Ross & Company, Inc., for compete business management of all its affairs.

In 1931, Beta Sigma Phi was a fairly simple organization. We had one degree, complicated and fairly difficult program work, one pin, and no magazine. The first issue of *The Torch*, the official magazine of Beta Sigma Phi, was only a four-page paper, sharing the news of the young sorority through its comparatively few chapters. It was published first in January of 1932, only nine months after the founding of the first chapter in Abilene. *The Torch* proved to be a powerful link among chapters, and quickly grew from a four-page bulletin to a magazine of thirty-two pages which regularly publishes stories and poems by members, personality sketches of various sisters and stories of our chapter's accomplishments. *The Torch* regularly runs contests for the membership, the most popular being our valentine contest, which is judged by a celebrity each year.

Just a few years after *The Torch* began, another great tradition, the Beta Sigma Phi convention, began as well. The first Beta Sigma Phi convention was held in Waterloo, Iowa on May 19 and 20, 1934. From that beginning, conventions soon began springing up everywhere, and now there is a convention each year in virtually every state in the United States, every province of Canada, and in Australia and Europe as well. Conventions are open to any member of Beta Sigma Phi.

Traditions soon spread though our chapters as well. The most important tradition of all grew out of the first year of sorority life. This is Founder's Day, which was celebrated for the first time on April 30, 1932. Another one of our most important traditions is the privilege of transfer. Members can transfer and feel as equally at home in a Beta Sigma Phi chapter in Canada as they would in the United States, or overseas. We have always been known for our remarkable ability to "do things right," and our founder's wife, Dorothy Ross, who supported her husband in many of his endeavors for the sorority, recalled the first reception held in Kansas City in 1933. She remembered that the members brought their own sandwiches and cakes and although beautifully dressed in their formal evening gowns, kept disappearing into the bathroom of the suite where the tea was being made! "They did things very well right from the beginning," Mrs. Ross said. "It's only the outward appearance that has changed."

There are a few things about Beta Sigma Phi which makes us different from other women's organizations. Our printed manuals and program outlines are all prepared especially for the sorority's exclusive use. Members moved by the depth and beauty of the rituals written for Beta Sigma Phi by the late Lynn Terry, one of the most influential members of the Beta Sigma Phi International Staff. All these publications come to members free of charge; they are included in the membership fee. The materials are constantly revised and brought up to date by Beta Sigma Phi's editorial staff, and they form the heart and core of the organization.

New ideas are a constant part of Beta Sigma Phi, and it was not long before the second degree of Beta Sigma Phi, which a member received upon the completion of pledge training, came into being. The first Ritual of Jewels degree was conferred upon Pennsylvania Beta Chapter of Harrisburg in November of 1933, and it became the official second degree.

Another historic occasion happened in 1935, when Beta Sigma Phi became international. Member Rilla Billings of California Alpha Eta, Oakland, moved to British Columbia, and took Beta sigma Phi with her! She started a chapter in her new home town and soon had the satisfaction of seeing that Beta Sigma Phi was just as acceptable on the north side of the longest undefended frontier in the world as it was on the south, and that it adapted itself readily to the needs of young women in Canada.

Since the establishment of that first chapter in Canada in 1935, chapters have been established throughout Canada, and in 30 other countries. Along with international growth came internal growth; city councils, which unite the chapters in a city and enable them to coordinate their activities, were meeting regularly in an ever-increasing number of cities by 1936.

It seemed that every year brought new ideas and excitement to our organization. At the urging of Donna Williams, whose mother, Marion Williams, was a charter member of Michigan Theta, Grand Rapids, a sorority for young women her own age was begun. In March of 1938, the first Nu Phi Mu chapter for girls under 21 was created. Membership carried the privilege of transferring to a Ritual of Jewels degree chapter of Beta Sigma Phi, and the first Nu Phi Mu graduated in this way in 1941.

Lynn Terry, who has been associated with Beta Sigma Phi from its beginning, became the president of Nu Phi Mu and held that office until 1953, when she retired to become head of the editorial board of Beta Sigma Phi. The business affairs of Nu Phi Mu were taken over by Walter W. Ross and company at that time. During the Silver Anniversary year, Nu Phi Mu officially became the first degree of Beta Sigma Phi, with all the same privileges and service as the chapters of higher degree.

By 1939, our ninth year of existence, the number of chapters reached the milestone of 1,000. A gift department was established at Beta Sigma Phi International to provide sorority jewelry not easily available anywhere else, and the International Staff of Beta Sigma Phi continued to grow. During that period in the late '30s International representatives were establishing new chapters in new towns throughout the United Stated and Canada. Virtually all new chapters came to Beta Sigma Phi during that time due to the untiring efforts of the International traveling staff. These women, selected and trained by Walter Ross, carried the banner of Beta Sigma Phi to great cities and small towns. All of us owe much to them for their great contributions to what was now the strength of Beta Sigma Phi throughout the world.

By 1940, another degree was formed, the Exemplar degree. This third degree of sorority was first conferred upon 12 members in Illinois Theta, Danville in 1940.

As the organization matured, service began to play a greater part in its activities. Beta Sigma Phi was not founded as a service organization; our first purposes were social and cultural in nature. The fact that so much service is done locally and internationally is a tribute to the character of the members. It was and is in their nature not only to give the best that is in them to themselves and their sorority, but to give the best that is in them to their world. World War II really brought Beta Sigma Phi into service work in a tremendous way.

It would be difficult, if not impossible, to find any good effort of that time in which Beta Sigma Phis were not involved. In 1944, over 1,000 Beta Sigma Phis were members of the armed services, serving in Canada, the United States, and overseas. Beta Sigma Phis received the United States Treasury Award for selling 22 million dollars worth of war bonds. In recognition of that wonderful record, Eleanor Roosevelt, who was an International Honorary member of Beta Sigma Phi, spoke at the Founder's Day observance in Washington D.C. (A list of all International Honorary Members will be supplied, at your request, from International.)

The war years were exciting years for Beta Sigma Phi. In 1941, the only international convention ever held for our members was organized in Kansas City, and members from throughout the organization attended this exciting occasion. We also launched our Beta Sigma Phi travel program and had the first "Ramble" to Canada.

In 1945, the war was barely over in Europe and was still going on in the South Pacific when Melita O'Hara, our Beta Sigma Phi travel counselor, went to Great Britain. She had the privilege of starting the first chapters of England and Scotland. Our international growth continued in the 1940s as chapters were formed in Tokyo, Germany, Austria, Finland and Greece.

In 1947, a very old friend invited Walter Ross to visit a laboratory at the University of Colorado where two dedicated scientists were struggling to continue their work in cancer research in the face of a gripping lack of funds. The fear that the work might have to cease altogether was ever present. And it seemed to the visitor as he was introduced to Dr. Margaret Kelsall and Dr. Edward Crabb that there was something here in which Beta Sigma Phi might be deeply and actively interested. He went home and wrote some letters about it.

The International Endowment Fund grew out of

that beginning, and was established in January of 1948. Beta Sigma Phi became the sole sponsor of the cancer research project, and continued its support for many years. In 1953, members extended their philanthropic activities to include regular donations to Girlstown U.S.A. in White-Face, Texas. Through the years a number of charitable, health and cultural foundations have received support from out International Endowment Fund. In 1955-56, chapters asked that a sum of $5,000 from that International Endowment Fund be given annually as a grant to a Canadian Project. This took the form of scholarships in English, scholarships in music, and an award to the author of a first outstanding Canadian novel. These awards and scholarships gave the greatest possible satisfaction to both the membership and the general public in Canada.

Through the years, the International Endowment Fund has continued to grow and accept additional projects. Contributions to all Beta Sigma Phi funds are voluntary.

Beta Sigma Phi from its beginning has been generous to others, and in November of 1951 the organization began to look after its own. This was done through the establishment of the International Loan Fund, which provides interest-free loans to members for emergencies arising out of illness or accident.

Reports are prepared and presented to the chapters at regular intervals on all the funds, including the Exemplar Fun, which for many years provided support for

Literacy Village in Lucknow, India, and now provides scholarships for members returning to education.

In 1955, the Order of the Rose was established to honor members of 15 or more years who had distinguished themselves within the organization of Beta Sigma Phi.

The Silver Anniversary year was celebrated from April 30, 1955 through April 30, 1956. It was a year memorable in many ways, by the formation of Silver Anniversary chapters and by the introduction of the achievement band with hearts for your years of membership and stars for your honors and offices. The opportunity to achieve paid-up status was also introduced during this year.

Another Silver Anniversary program instituted was the legacy program, which offers special memberships to Beta Sigma Phi daughters, granddaughters, nieces and other young girls special to our present members. Future Beta Sigma Phis can now be enrolled at International before their 18th birthday by these members. The money deposited at International for this little girl, will, through interest earned in this account, have her membership fees paid in full by the time she reaches the age of initiation into a Beta Sigma Phi chapter. A beautiful symbol was created for these young Beta Sigma Phis to treasure through the years before their pledgeship in Beta Sigma Phi. It is a beautiful necklace with a rosebud pendant bearing the Greek letters of the organization.

The Preceptor degree, the fourth degree of our sorority, was announced in 1959, and the first Preceptor chapter was established in Pocatello, Idaho. By 1960, Beta Sigma Phi has grown to a membership of 150,000 members with 7,000 chapters in 14 countries.

The International Office of Beta Sigma Phi had moved several times as the organization grew and more space was required for the staff. Now the International Office has its own building at 1800 West 91st Place in Kansas City, Missouri 64114. The office occupies a specially designed three-story red brick building which was constructed in 1962. Hundreds of members visit the office each year, and every member is welcome. About 30 persons are employed in the office on a full-time basis. Members of the staff always have time to answer questions, show visitors around, and introduce them to the rest of our staff. A visit gives you an opportunity to watch how we handle the more than one million pieces of mail that are processed through the International office each year.

When Walter Ross died in 1969, a number of memorials for our founder were suggested. One that would have met with his complete approval was selected and established. A Walter W. Ross Memorial Scholarship Fund was set up to provide college scholarships for children and grandchildren of members. The fund has provided thousands of scholarships for students since its beginning, and scholarships are awarded by a committee independent of the International Office staff.

In 1974, the Laureate degree, our fifth degree, was

announced. The first Laureate chapter was established in Centralia, Illinois. The following years that have included our Golden Anniversary (and many new Golden Anniversary chapters), the creation of our Master degree (in 1988, formed in Kansas City, Missouri), the and our 60th anniversary in 1991 and the creation of the Torchbearer degree in 2012 have been full, rewarding years for the membership. They are just part of a long and proud history of Beta Sigma Phi, one that you will add your own footnotes to, in the days to come.

The next lesson will discuss your International Office. Please read that section and be prepared to discuss it.

Questions for Seventh Meeting

1. Who founded Beta Sigma Phi?

2. Where and when was the first chapter of Beta Sigma Phi founded?

3. Why was the name "Beta Sigma Phi" chosen?

4. Where is the International office?

5. When is Founder's Day celebrated each year?

6. What is the official monthly publication of Beta Sigma Phi?

7. What is the International Endowment Fund and how is it used?

8. What is the International Loan Fund and how is it used?

9. Who may be enrolled as a Legacy Member?

10. Scholarship application forms are mailed to each chapter each year. Who may apply for a scholarship?

Eighth Meeting

INVITATION TO LIFE

YOUR INTERNATIONAL OFFICE

Beta Sigma Phi is a nonprofit corporation which maintains a contract with Walter W. Ross & Company, Incorporated, for complete business management of all its affairs.

1. FORMATION OF CHAPTERS. The International Executive Council determines when and where new chapters may be organized. After permission to organize has been secured from the Executive Council new chapters may be organized:

a. By Friendly Venture. This is when an existing chapter, council, or member organizes a new chapter to be composed mostly of new members.

b. By progression. This is when members of one degree are eligible to progress to a higher degree and form a new chapter of that higher degree.

c. By transferees. This is when transferees from various communities get together to form a chapter.

A new chapter may be installed with a membership of ten or more.

2. HOW CHAPTERS ARE NAMED. The International Executive Council assigns a chapter name and number when the names of the members who will compose the new chapter (with pledge agreements when needed) and the names of the first slate of officers are

recieved.

Ritual of Jewels chapter names: The first such chapter in each state is Alpha, the second Beta, and so on through the Greek alphabet to Omega. Then double names are used, as Alpha Alpha, Alpha Beta, and so forth.

Other degrees: As with the Ritual of Jewels chapters, chapters of other degrees are named in Greek alphabetical order with a prefix to designate the degree. The prefixes are: Phi to indicate a Nu Phi Mu chapter; Xi to indicate an Exemplar chapter; Preceptor, Laureate and Torchbearer chapters use the full title of the degree before the chapter name. Master chapters list chapter name first, then the title Master.

Members should always know and use their current chapter number as well as chapter name. Just as there is a prefix in front of the chapter name to indicate the degree (except in the case of Ritual of Jewels chapters) there is a letter prefix in front of the chapter number to indicate the degree. Nu Phi Mu degree chapters have the prefix "NP" in front of their chapter number; "EX" indicates Exemplar chapters; "XP" indicates Preceptor chapters; "PL" indicates Laureate chapters; "MA" indicates Master degree chapters, and "TO" indicates Torchbearer chapters. Thus, from the chapter number as well as from the chapter name, the degree of a chapter is easily identified.

3. THE TORCH. Your International Office is responsible for the publication of the official magazine of

Beta Sigma Phi, *The Torch*. Published 7 times annually, *The Torch* provides a connecting link between active members, all of whom receive the electronic edition as part of their membership, and provides information and special features of interest to Beta Sigma Phis. A subcription to the lovely, colorful print edition is available to members at only $14 per year.

All Beta Sigma Phi contests are announced and outlined in detail in *The Torch* in advance of each deadline and winners are announced in *The Torch*. The following contests are open to all Beta Sigma Phis in good standing:

Poetry Contest - deadline, postmarked by May 1. Entry must be original, unpublished, on any theme, and of any length.

Valentine Contest - deadline, postmarked by November 1. A hard-copy photograph of the chapter's Valentine Queen should be submitted to the Inernational Office by November 1. The Valentine contest is judged by a celebrity or other noteworthy personality and the winner apepars on the cover of the February issue of *The Torch*.

Yearbook Contest - deadline, postmarked by November 15. Chapters may submit an entry identical to the yearbook the chapter's members will be using during the current chapter year. The yearbooks should include planning for stimulation of interest and participation in programs, socials, service, ways and means; a roster of members, committees, and officers; also a calendar of chapter activities.

Photo Contest - deadline, postmarked by May 1. Entries must be original and submitted by Beta Sigma Phis in good standing. Your photo subject(s) should be Beta Sigma Phi related. One non-returnable photo (color or black and white) can be submitted per member.

Spring Parade of Legacies - Many Legacies are pictured each year in the Spring and Fall Parade of Legacies in the May-June and September-October issues of *The Torch*. One non-returnable photo can be submitted of each legacy (legacy only - no member or group photos).

The International Office of Beta Sigma Phi is loctaed at 1800 West 91st Place, Kansas City, Missouri, 64114. The office is open five days a week, year-round, and members are always welcome.

We cannot overemphasize the importance of having your full name, address, and your chapter number on all of your correspondence. Every month some 40,000 changes are made to membership records. A member may write or email the International Office if she has a question, or when she wishes to put her enjoyment of Beta Sigma Phi into words. Knowing how she enjoys her membership, or how they can help her enjoy it more, is a real reward to the members of your International Staff.

The door of the President's office usually stands wide open, and there is an instant feeling of welcome and being made, so to speak, one of the family. Nobody's problems are too small or unimportant for her to share.

The next meeting discusses the structure of Beta Sigma Phi. Please read the mateiral and be ready to discuss it.

Questions for Eighth Meeting

1. The International Office is open every month of the year. Who may visit the International Office? When?

2. What is the address of the International Office?

3. Name the contests that require chapter participation.

4. Which contests are open to every individual member?

Ninth Meeting

INVITATION TO LIFE

STRUCTURE OF BETA SIGMA PHI

All chapters of Beta Sigma Phi meet regularly and closely follow the calendar suggested by International. All members and chapters adhere to the International Constitution of *Beta Sigma Phi.* This can be found in the Book of Beta Sigma Phi. The index in the back of the book will guide you to any specific point. The following questions will help to guide your discussion; other questions will suggest themselves.

a. What is the object of Beta Sigma Phi set forth in the Constitution?

b. What is the structure of Beta Sigma Phi?

c. What are powers of the International organization?

d. What composes the membership?

e. What is the Executive Council?

In addition to the International Constitution of Beta Sigma Phi, each chapter composes its own set of bylaws. These bylaws, when approved by the International Executive Council, provide the framework for the individual chapters. In an established chapter, the pledges should review the chapter bylaws and become familiar with them. In a new chapter, the pledges should compose their own set of chapter bylaws, adhering as closely as possible to the Suggested Chapter Bylaws that can be found in the *Book of Beta Sigma Phi.*

Another good source is the *President's Guidebook*, in the chapter box of supplies. If you need another copy, you can purchase one from International.

At this point the plege should be familiar with the Rules and Regulations for the Governance of Members and Chapters, the Chapter Constitution and Bylaws of Beta Sigma Phi, and the Standing rules, all found in the *Book of Beta Sigma Phi.* Let the following questions be a guide for your discussions.

a. What is the object of a chapter?

b. What are the qualifications for a charter?

c. What attendance is required from each member? What is an excused absense?

d. Name the offices of a chapter.

e. How are officers elected?

f. Who composes the Executive Board and what are its duties?

g. When is a member in good standing?

h. When are membership cards issued?

i. How and why are members declared inactive?

j. What is required to transfer to another chapter of the same degree? What is required to reinstate to active membership?

K. What fees are there and who determines them? What are the amounts?

l. What are Councils? How are they formed? What is their purpose?

m. What are the social functions held each year?

BETA SIGMA PHI PLEDGE REVIEW

Use these questions (we have provided an answer key for the pledge trainer) to be sure training has been thorough, and pledges have a good understanding of Beta Sigma Phi. If 90% of the pledge class earns scores of 80% or more, your pledges will receive a special certificate of recognition!

BETA SIGMA PHI PLEDGE REVIEW

1. Who is the founder of Beta Sigma Phi?

2. When (month/day/year) and where was Beta Sigma Phi founded?

3. How was the name "Beta Sigma Phi" chosen?

4. The two main statuses of membership in Beta Sigma Phi are active membership and inactive membership. List the three types of active membership and briefly explain each, and explain inactive membership.

5. Only one of the following is eligible for chapter honorary membership. Circle the correct response.
   A. A woman who has never been pledged into Beta Sigma Phi.
   B. Husbands.
   C. Inactive members of Beta Sigma Phi.

6. Name the three types of chapter honorary membership (not required, but can you explain the differences?).

7. There are over _____ members of Beta Sigma Phi in approximately _____ chapters in _____ countries.

8. How are Beta Sigma Phi charters named?

9. What is your chapter's proper name?

10. What is your personal member number?

11. Who can be an International Honorary Member?

12. Name two sorority traditions.

13. What is the official magazine entitled?

14. What are the colors of Beta Sigma Phi?

15. What is the flower of Beta Sigma Phi?

16. What is the Latin motto of Beta Sigma Phi? What does it mean?

17. Briefly explain the purpose of each of the International Funds.

18. Name the officers of your chapter and briefly explain their duties (a chapter can have 4-6 officers).

19. What is the official manual for Beta Sigma Phi?

20. What is the "test for membership" in Beta Sigma Phi?

21. How may a decision of the Executive Board be changed?

22. If one of the officers is unable to complete her term of office, how is the vacancy filled?

23. Can pledges hold office?

24. Name the seven degrees of Beta Sigma Phi, in order, and how many years of active chapter participation and cultural program work is needed in each, in order to become eligible for progression to the next degree.

25. How does a member become eligible for the Order of the Rose?

26. What is the Silver Circle? The Golden Circle? The Diamond Circle?

27. Legacy membership refers to (circle the correct response):

A. Pledging a friend in your chapter.

B. Enrolling a girl, before the age of 18, in Beta Sigma Phi.

C. Inactive members who wish to affiliate with a chapter.

28. Where is the International Office located?

29. When is Founder's Day?

30. When is Beginning Day (traditionally) each year?

31. Who may apply for the Walter and Dorothy Ross Memorial Scholarships?

32. Write the Greek letter symbols for Beta Sigma Phi and for your chapter.

33. What is the privilege of transfer?

34. Name four annual contests sponsored by Beta Sigma Phi International.

35. Have you memorized the Opening and Closing Rituals? This is part of the pledge review.

36. In your own words, what is the purpose of Beta Sigma Phi?

ANSWER KEY FOR PLEDGE REVIEW
1. Walter W. Ross.

2. April 30, 1931 - Abilene, Kansas.

3. Names after the Greek words meaning Life, Learning, and Friendship. The Greek letters Beta, Sigma and Phi begin these three words.

4. A) Active - current in payment of both International fees, chapter dues and fully participating in a chapter. B) Leave of Absense - having approval of chapter to be absent from chapter meetings and activities for a period of up to one year. Must be in payment of International fees. C) Member-at large - current in payment of International fees, but having no chapter affiliation. D) Inactive Membership - not current in payment of International fees. Not participating in a chapter.

5. A: A woman who has never been pledged into Beta Sigma Phi.

6. Honorary member, sponsor, director.
7. 150,000; 10,000; more than 10.

8. In Greek alphabetical order within each state. Nu Phi Mu chapters have "Phi" at the beginning of each chapter name; Exemplar chapters have "Xi" at the beginning of each chapter name; Preceptor chapter names are preceded by the word "Preceptor"; Laureate chapters have the word "Laureate" preceding the Greek letters; Master chapters all include the word "Master;" Torchbearer chapter names are preceded by the word "Torchbearer," and Ritual of Jewels chapter names just follow the Greek alphabet - i.e., Alpha, Beta, etc.

9. (Example) Missouri Omega, Kansas City

10. Your member number.

11. A woman who is known nationally and/or internationally for her outstanding achievements and who is recommended to the International Executive Council by a city council or chapter, and approved by IEC.

12. Any from those listed in the Book of Beta Sigma Phi would be accetable as a correct answer.

13. *The Torch* of Beta Sigma Phi.

14. Black and Gold.

15. Yellow rose.

16. Vita Scientia Amicitia (Vita meaning life, Scientia meaning learning, and Amicitia meaning friendship).

17. A) International Endowment Fund - monies contributed by chapters, councils and members as contributions to be given to various service and charitable organizations that have been approved by the membership. B) International Exemplar Fund - monies contributed by chapters, councils, and members to be used for scholarships for members, chosen through a judging process once a year. C) Dorothy and Walter Ross Scholarship Fund - scholarships of $1,000 each awarded yearly to children or grandchildren of members in good standing. The number of scholarships granted each year depends on the earnings of the Scholarship Fund. D) The International Loan Fund - Emergency loans to members and close family in case of illness or injury.

18. A) President; B) Vice-President; C) Recording Secretary; D) Corresponding Secretary; E) Treasurer; F) Extension Officer

19. The *Book of Beta Sigma Phi*.

20. The handshake; a member says "Beta Sigma Phi"; other member says "I am thy sister."

21. By a two-thirds vote of the members at a regular or special meeting of the chapter with a quorum present.

22. By appointment of another member to the office by the Chapter Executive Board.

23. Yes.

24. A) Nu Phi My - three years; B) Ritual of Jewels - four years; C) Exemplar - six years; D) Preceptor - eight years; E) Laureate - ten years; F) Master - 12 years; G) Torchbearer.

25. By being active in chapters for 15 complete years (or, if an honorary member, by holding that position for the same length of time); by being active in a chapter above the Ritual of Jewels degree; and, by being notable for her fidelity to the ideals of Beta Sigma Phi, by her industry, and for her loyal dedication to the organization throughout the entire period of her membership.

26. These are celebrations to recognize years of membership - 25 active years for the Silver Circle, 50 years since pledging for the Golden Circle, and 60 years since pledging for the Diamond Circle.

27. B. Enrolling a girl, before the age of 18, in Beta Sigma Phi.

28. Kansas City, Missouri.

29. April 30 of each year.

30. The last Sunday of August

31. Members and children and grandchidren of members.

32. ΒΣΦ.

33. Any member in good standing may transfer to another chapter of her degree upon notification to International in approval of such transfer by a majority vote of the chapter she is joining.

34. Yearbook, Valentine, Photo, Poetry.

Did 90% of your pledge class earn scores of 80% or more; on this review? If so, please tell your International division chairman, so she can send your pledge class its certificate of recognition!

THE GREEK ALPHABET

Alpha	A
Beta	B
Gamma	Γ
Delta	Δ
Epsilon	E
Zeta	Z
Eta	H
Theta	Θ
Iota	I
Kappa	K
Lambda	Λ
Mu	M
Nu	N
Xi	Ξ
Omicron	O
Pi	Π
Rho	P
Sigma	Σ
Tau	T
Upsilon	Υ
Phi	Φ
Chi	X
Psi	Ψ
Omega	Ω

PRONUNCIATION GUIDE
FOR GREEK ALPHABET

Note that every "a" on the end of a word is pronounced as in the word "above."

Alpha: Al - as in the man's name Al. Pha as in fa (above). Al'pha.

Beta: Be - as in Bay, ta (above). Be'ta.

Gamma: Gam - as in am, Ma (above). Gam'ma.

Delta: Del - as in Bell, ta. Delt'ta.

Epsilon: Ep - as in Epsom salts, Si as in sick, Lon as in long. Ep'si'lon.

Zeta: Ze - as in day, ta. Ze'ta.

Eta: E - as in day (the E becomes ay), ta. E'ta.

Theta: Th - as in thought, e as in day, ta. The'ta.

Iota: I - as in I, o as in oh, ta. I'o'ta.

Kappa: Kap - as in cap, pa. Kap'pa.

Lambda: Lamb as in the word lamb, da. Lamb'da.

Mu: Just as in the word you with an M in front of it. Mu.

Nu: Just as the word you with an N in front of it. Nu.

Xi: Ze - as in zoo, i as in I. Xi.

Omicron: Om as in awe with an m ending, i as in it, kron as in on. Om'i'kron.

Pi: Pi - as in the word pie. Pi.

Rho: Rho - as in the word row. Rho.

Simga: Sig - as in cigarette, ma. Sig'ma.

Tau: Tau - as in talk, but drop the lk. Tau.

Upsilon: Up - as in the word oops, si as in sick, lon as in long. U'p'si'lon.

Phi: Phi - as in fight, dropping the ght. Phi.

Chi: Chi - as in kite, dropping the te. Chi.

Psi: prounounced just like the word sign, dropping the n. Psi.

Omega: O - as in oh, me as in May, ga (above). O'me'ga.

"Why don't you take your badge at the start of
each day, name the colors for the six jewels.
Red...yellow...blue...orange...
green...and violet.
Then touch each jewel with the affirmation
of courage...vision...humility...loyalty...
fellowship...and service.

"Whenever you do that you will have added to
your life a little more courage, vision, humility, a
little more loyalty, fellowship and service. And as
often as you do that you will have given the
world a little more courage, vision, humility,
a little more loyalty, friendship and service."

Walter W. Ross, Founder

Made in the USA
Coppell, TX
17 May 2024

32516716R00066